'The Vraic or Sea-weed Harvest, Guernsey', as published in the *Illustrated London News*, 11 September 1852. The scene is at Rocquaine, with Fort Grey and the heights of Pleinmont in the distance. In the foreground are carts laden with seaweed, some of them drawn by oxen. Also visible are horses with panniers, in which the *vraic* was carried from shore to farm. It was then spread onto the fields as a fertiliser; originally, it was also burnt for fuel. In the past, *vraic* was so valuable to farmers that its gathering was restricted by ordinance, except when it was washed ashore, when it could be gathered at any time. Cutting the seaweed, however, was only allowed at certain times of the year. Nowadays, hardly any is used on the fields and a scene such as this will not be seen again.

OLD GUERNSEY
In Pictures

Tomato-picking, *c.*1960.

OLD GUERNSEY
In Pictures

including
Alderney, Sark, Herm, Jethou and Lihou

Victor Coysh
and
Carel Toms

Phillimore

1989

Published by
PHILLIMORE & CO. LTD.,
Shopwyke Hall, Chichester, Sussex

© Victor Coysh and Carel Toms, 1989

ISBN 0 85033 711 9

Printed and bound in Great Britain by
BIDDLES LTD.,
Guildford, Surrey

List of Illustrations

Frontispiece: Tomato-picking, *c*.1960

Acknowledgements

The authors are most grateful to those people who were kind enough to lend several photographs, without which this book would have been much the poorer. They include members of the Alderney Society, Messrs. E. B. Best, Rex Bragg, S. Budge, Roy Falla, E. Guille, J. Middlebrook, S. A. Noel, S. Simon, F. Zabiela, J. Goodwin and A. Heyworth, Mrs. H. Hamon, Mrs. C. M. Trufitt, Major A. G. Wood, the Guernsey Press, the Priaulx and Guille-Allès Libraries and Millard & Co. Ltd.

Introduction

This is the fourth volume of photographic memories of the Bailiwick. In the three previous books, *Guernsey Through the Lens*, *Guernsey Through the Lens Again* and *Bygone Guernsey*, we brought together some 600 photographs showing the diversity of life in these islands in almost every field of activity.

From the inception of photography in the 1850s, the camera has captured images of ourselves and our environment which are constant reminders that Guernsey and the neighbouring islands have changed. In St Peter Port, one is far more likely to see people in business suits carrying brief cases, than fishermen clad in guernseys and shouldering *poniers*.

The motor car, jet aircraft, television, radio and other innovations have changed our lives. Old industries have folded up as new ones have been born; over-population and over-development are now with us in this present age of prosperity and the way of life which our fathers and forefathers enjoyed has gone for ever.

Photographs such as those we have assembled here are further reflections from our past. Some are of people who have served us well; others are of once familiar places which have changed beyond all recognition or even vanished completely.

We would like to pay tribute to all those who keep old photographs and particularly those who were happy to loan them for reproduction so that their treasured records could be seen by a wider audience.

Victor Coysh and Carel Toms

The Plates

St Peter Port

1. Castle Cornet as it appeared in about 1860. This early photograph was taken from the vicinity of Les Côtils and shows the castle without its breakwater. On the right is the eastern flank of the castle emplacement, upon which the Model Yacht Pond was later built. The general appearance of the fortress has hardly changed and the Union flag still flies from the summit of the castle.

2. Le Grand Carrefour or, as it is more commonly known, 'the top of High Street'. This photograph was taken in about 1910, when E. J. Harris had his grocery business there. In the window are advertisements typical of the period and the shop's old-fashioned appearance matched that of its neighbour, H. J. Cumber, partially seen on the left. W. J. Powell's premises were more ornate, since this wine merchant traded in part of the former Brock family residence, later to become the *Royal Yacht Hotel* and now occupied by Boots. Its granite façade is most handsome and today it bears a plaque stating that Maj. Gen. Sir Isaac Brock once lived there.

3.   The New Jetty as it appeared on 16 May 1928. The accepted tender for its construction was £110,743, not including the offices and other buildings which were added later. The jetty is 600 ft. long on one side and 685 ft. on the other. Its width is 155 ft. and it has a floor space of approximately two and a half acres. The photograph shows the submarines H23 and L11, with their depot ship H.M.S. *Alecto*. Later, the submarines entered the harbour and were visited by many islanders.

4.   The Guernsey Swimming Club aquatic carnival was held on 9 July 1932. The Great Western Railway Company's booking offices and refreshment rooms, seen in the background, were demolished in 1935. The photograph was taken from the jetty and the spectacle was enjoyed by the hundreds visible in the picture.

Ladies' Bathing Place, Guernsey.

5. The ladies' bathing place, as this feature of La Vallette used to be called. The area reserved for gentlemen was located a discreet distance away. Very few seem to be bathing when this early photograph was taken, although the presence of towels on either side of the buildings suggests that the ladies in the picture had already had a decorous 'dip'. The idea of sunbathing was unknown then and those posing for the photographer seem to be very over-dressed by modern standards. In the background are the heights of Les Terres, now much more wooded than they used to be. Today this is a mixed pool, something unheard of when this postcard was printed.

6. At first glance, it may not be easy to identify this view, *c.*1880. The buildings comprise the rear aspect of shops in Le Pollet, as seen from the sea front. The trees on the left were growing in a plantation, most of which is now covered by the States Office, built in 1911. In fact, this part of old St Peter Port remains much as it used to be, although the wares sold in the shops are very different. Mr. C. Foster no longer sells tin plate and articles made of zinc.

Smith Street, *c.*1910. Superficially, it looks much the same today, apart from Boots the Chemists, whose premises on ̣e right were transferred in the 1920s to a building at the bottom of Smith Street, then the *Royal Yacht Hotel*. Another ̣ference, of course, is the Edwardian style of dress. Traffic is absent in this summer scene and even nowadays it is ̣latively scarce in Smith Street.

In 1935 the condition of Cornet Street was deplorable and the States resolved to demolish several of its buildings. This ̣otograph shows the desolate scene near the top of the hill. In due course, buildings in fair condition were restored, ̣t much of the street now comprises pleasing plantations in place of slums.

9.   The fish market is always attractive, especially to visitors, but when it was decorated on the scale to be seen in this photograph the sight must indeed have been remarkable. It was decorated for Christmas in the 1930s and, when the gas lamps were alight, the sight must have been particularly enchanting.

10.   The weighbridge building faced the Picquet House at the South Esplanade and was replaced by an electricity sub-station. The ornamental slab in the foreground was the back of a granite horse trough, which has been upturned very near its original site. Subsequently, public conveniences were added to the building. This photograph was taken before the tram service between town and St Sampson's ended in 1934. An advertisement outside the kiosk indicates that a certain brand of Bucktrout's cigarettes cost 7d. for twenty.

11.   In October 1935, the Great Western Railway's booking offices, refreshment rooms and stores at the White Rock were demolished. They had been built in 1892. The coigns and lintels were numbered and some of them were used for the extension of the Albert Pier weighbridge, when it was reconstructed as an electricity supply sub-station in 1937, situated close to the present bus station.

12.   This photograph, taken in about 1930, shows part of St Pete
Port under snow, with a threatening sky forming a dramatic
background. Fort George can be seen on the skyline whilst
St Barnabas church, now empty but once a museum, is in the
centre. To the left of it is Ozanne Hall, with part of Fountain Street
in the foreground. The picture was probably taken from the vicinit
of Constitution Steps.

13.   Cambridge Park wearing a winter coat. The depth of the snow
can be appreciated by observing the legs of the pedestrians and the
dog. The trees present a remarkably lovely picture and the severity
of the snowfall was sufficiently great for it to be the subject of a
Guernsey Evening Press picture taken in pre-war times.

. The saluting battery at Castle Cornet as it was in 1939. Old cannon fired salutes on auspicious occasions such as the
vereign's birthday and this still occurs today, albeit on a modified scale. At the curtain battery (east of the saluting
ttery) the midday gun is fired in the summer and on the Queen's birthday it is joined by neighbouring cannon in firing
alute. The old guns of Castle Cornet were removed by the Germans during the Occupation and after Liberation they
re more or less replaced from various sources. Today the saluting battery of the past is filled mostly with replicas of
h-century guns.

The White Hart public house in this picture was demolished in 1974 and has since been rebuilt as *The Waterfront*,
hough part of it is still named 'White Hart'. Originally it was *St Julian's Hotel*, whose proprietor was Charles Newbury.
wever, its best known licensee was Edward Henry Zabiela, who held the licence from 1928 until 1942, when the German
cupiers of Guernsey turned him out. The pub was cleverly converted into part of Hitler's 'impregnable fortress'.
ndows became gun ports and the bunker housed the means of blowing up the harbour installations in the event of an
ack. Fortunately, this never happened and the occupiers surrendered on 9 May 1945. During the redevelopment of the
a in 1975, Bernie Griffin raised the *Clameur de Haro* (an ancient island custom which has the effect of halting all work
til the matter is resolved in the Royal Court) against the use of a crane with a 98-ft. jib which moved across the air space
ove his property in the Lower Pollet.

16. On 4 June 1944, when Fort George was a German fortress, the R.A.F. attacked it with rockets and gunfire. The guard room clock inside the main gate stopped at 5.25p.m., the time at which the raid took place. In 1969 the guard room was demolished and the old clock was acquired by Mr.G.C. Archer, who built a house at Fort Irwin. He installed it on a wall of the fort and reset the time to ten minutes to five as he felt the hands would not look so good if they were overlapping.

17. St Julian's Avenue was laid out in 1870 and the elm trees which flanked it were once the pride of Guernsey. The trees – then some eighty years old – had become rotten and unsafe, and in 1949 they were felled. In 1950 the States decided to replant the avenue with Norwegian maples at the lower end and flowering trees at the top. This photograph shows trees being replanted in that year. All the buildings in the background, including that of C. P. Kinnell and Co. Ltd., greenhouse heating engineers, have vanished. From 1980 onwards, they were replaced by several banking premises: Lazard House (which constitutes the corner at the bottom), Hamilton House, Hambro House, St Julian's Court and Bermuda House (on the site of the former Gaumont cinema, demolished in 1985). As for the trees planted in 1950, they too were replaced, this time by Swedish whitebeam.

18.   Not long after this photograph was taken in 1968, *The Sussex* public house closed down. One publican associated with this establishment was T. H. (Tommy) Zabiela, brother of Ted Zabiela who ran *The White Hart* near the weighbridge. Tommy retired in 1953. During the late 19th century the building was run as *Hotel de l'Europe* by George Mace.

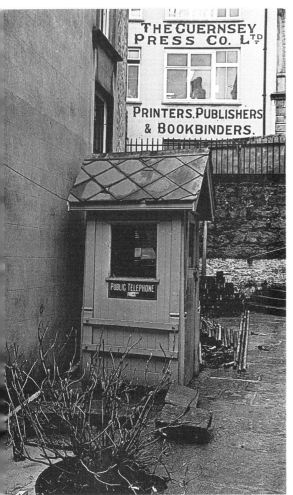

19.   When the medieval buildings in Smith Street were demolished to make way for 19th-century development, most of the street (also known as Rue des Forges) was swept away. The *Guernsey Evening Press* Company moved to the street from Le Pollet in 1900 and later acquired and built new premises at Le Marchant Street (which runs parallel with Smith Street). This is believed to be the site of the forge which gave the street its name. The building housed the company's printing works until they were moved to the Braye Road, Vale, in 1979, after 62 years in St Peter Port. The old-style telephone kiosk seen here was replaced by a modern version in 1970.

20.   What is now the premises of the C. I. Co-operative Society Ltd. used to be the gentlemen's outfitting business of A. F. Cox. Originally the building was known as Rectory House, since the rector of St Peter Port once resided there. In its day it housed a cinema (Rectory Hall) on its first floor and not so long ago there was also a café upstairs. The photograph was taken in 1961.

21.   This is how the lower part of St James' Street looked in 1954. It was a small public garden at the foot of which was a tiny police station. A new police headquarters was built on this site in 1955. Part of the building now houses the offices of Her Majesty's Procureur (H.M. Attorney-General) and H.M. Comptroller (H.M. Solicitor-General). Having expanded still further, the police headquarters is to move once again. The former St Peter Port Hospital in Hospital Lane is now being converted for this purpose.

22.   *Les Caves de Bordeaux* public house once had a unique row
of 15 casks of wine and spirits behind the bar which were
placed there by the pub's founder, M. Giles Feuillerat, in
1884. Each held 240 gallons. After stocks ran out during
1941, when the Germans were in occupation, the barrels were
never used again. The fronts, bearing names like Eau de Vie,
Demerara Rum, Old Schiedam, Marsala and Fino Sherry,
were placed in front of the bar. M. Feuillerat came to
Guernsey from the French Basque country and was an
itinerant pedler. His son, Bertin, built the premises in 1884.
M. A. Bulteau followed as owner and when he died in 1930,
the pub was purchased by Mackay and Co. Ltd. The picture
shows George Gould beside one of the barrels when they
stood in their original position.

23.   Few buildings in the heart of St Peter Port have entirely
escaped redevelopment. The Guernsey Stamp Shop and
Warry's bakery and confectionery shop were two ancient
Pollet Street premises which were demolished and rebuilt in
the 1960s.

24. The appearance of the St Julian's weighbridge area of St Peter Port has considerably altered since the demolition and rebuilding of the surrounding premises. Growers' agents George Monro, the Chicken Platter Takeaway and Julian S. Hodge occupied these premises before they were demolished in 1974 and replaced by Manufacturers Hanover House and Lazard House. The weighbridge itself, which is owned by the States, dated from 1892 and is now the office of Central Taxis.

25. The best known building in New Street (Rue Marguerite) was the Lyric Theatre. Since this photograph was taken in 1974, this side of the street has been replaced by offices and flats. The Lyric was originally a non-conformist chapel built in the 19th century and rebuilt as a theatre, complete with horseshoe balcony. The stage, however, was too small to be used for any serious dramatic productions. It then became a cinema but, when the Germans occupied the island in 1940, it was closed. It soon became a mecca for those interested in amateur dramatics and thousands of people were entertained there throughout the war. When the island was liberated, it was used as a cinema by British Forces. In 1951 it was converted into a billiards hall but was finally closed down in about 1977. Soon after the war, the States took an interest in the building and in 1947 appointed the Arts Investigation Committee. As a result they purchased the Lyric for £3,250 and 1949 saw the birth of an Arts Committee, set up to 'promote interest in arts and crafts ... and to administer the Lyric and Arts Centre, when established'. In 1950, however, the States decided that it would be 'uneconomic' to go ahead with the conversion, which would have cost £8,000, and the premises were sold.

26. This old pump stood in the Bordage, facing the foot of Tower Hill. Made of cast iron, it bore its original date of 1871 as well as the names of De La Cour and Guilbert, St Peter Port constables, together with those holding office in 1919, Messrs. Murdoch and Mauger. Unfortunately the pump, a rarity of its type, was removed about thirty years ago.

Coast & Country

27. *Le Gouffre Hotel*, about a century ago. It was a substantial building, much frequented by visitors arriving in four-in-hand excursion cars, as well as by residents in quest of a peaceful holiday. A form of marquee can be seen on the left and the small buildings facing it still survive today, although the hotel does not. It was almost destroyed during the German Occupation and its ruins were cleared away afterwards to make way for the present restaurant. The fisherman on the path has probably returned from the little harbour at La Moye, where he may have kept his boat. Today, the area is more overgrown with vegetation than in 1890.

28. A lively event in the Rocquaine Regatta, photographed in the early years of the present century. This was a race for fishing craft and these typical Guernsey-built boats under sail make a striking picture. Most of those shown are mackerel boats, a larger version of the crabber. The former fared further afield than those engaged chiefly in inshore fishing. Today fishing is an important industry, but the vessels used are very much larger than the sailing boats of yesterday and, most will agree, they are certainly not as attractive.

29. Mrs. Marquand, formerly Miss Betsy Duquemin, ran a small school behind Roseland House in the Landes du Marché. This photograph shows Mrs. Marquand, in the centre, together with pupils and helpers.

30. Roseland House, which stands opposite Shiloh church in the Landes du Marché. The two people in the centre are Mr. and Mrs. John Marquand.

31. In 1964, lean-to greenhouses were not uncommon. These principals, however, are much rarer. They were former ships' masts and extend from ground level to the roof. This greenhouse once grew vines, as the apertures in the low stone wall reveal, but this crop was freesias. The building, owned by Mr. George Le Couteur, stood on the Rocquaine coast road.

32. One of the great attractions of the past for visitors to Guernsey was the Long House at Longfield Vinery in Guelles Road, St Peter Port. It was owned by Mr. P. Gallienne, whose 750-ft. long vinery produced some 25,000 bunches of grapes each year. The grapes usually ripened during August, September and October, and for 5s., 7s. 6d. or 10s. Mr. Gallienne would send baskets of grapes to any part of the British Isles within 36 hours.

33. Best's brickfield in St Andrew's as it was in 1900. Glasshouse stood beside the works, and a kiln is visible near the windmill, which also featured in the manufacture of bricks. The photograph shows men and boys employed in the industry; behind them, a boxcart and horse are visible. Although bricks are no longer made here, the premises have changed very little.

34. The Vale Avenue Methodist church, otherwise known as the Vale Avenue United Methodist chapel, was opened in 1910. In 1918 it became a cinema and after 1960 it was converted into a garage by Stanley A. Noel Ltd.

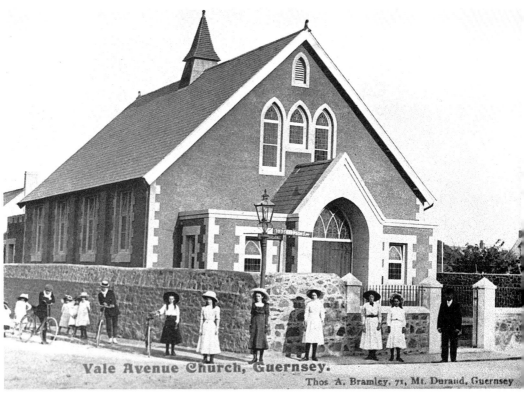

Vale Avenue Church, Guernsey.

Thos. A. Bramley, 71, Mt. Durand, Guernsey.

5. In about 1916 work began on the renovation of the Vale Methodist chapel. Amongst those who assisted were, from left to right: (*front row*) Rex Bragg, Nellie Ingrouille, Minnie Ingrouille, Nellie Way (née Bowen); (*rear row*) Frank Bragg, Mr. Washington, Bertha Way (née Blondel), Miss Downie, –, Mrs. Washington and Dolly Downie.

36. The Vale Avenue garage.

37. At a time when corn was grown on a large scale in Guernsey, windmills such as the one at Le Coudré, St Pierre du Bois, were a common sight. When this photograph was taken, the windmill had become a mere shell, for its working days were long past. The tower became a sea-mark and was duly white-washed for this purpose, standing on a hillside overlooking Rocquaine Bay. Unhappily, it was destroyed during the German Occupation. On the right of the picture is Mr. George Ralls, leader of the 1st Guernsey Scouts who camped near the mill in the 1930s.

38. La Maison du Neuf Chemin, St Saviour's, as it appeared in 1938. Soon afterwards this fine old house, together with several others, was abandoned when the reservoir flooded. On completion, the reservoir was able to hold 241 million gallons of water. Work on its construction began in the summer of 1938 but the German Occupation delayed operations and it was not completed until 1947. It took only three months to fill the reservoir, thanks to a wet winter and high snowfall that year. At first, the newly-constructed reservoir and mighty dam gave a raw appearance to the area, but today the reservoir is once again a place of beauty. When the water level is very low, the ruins of the buildings which once stood there become visible.

39. This scene, although very familiar in 1937, is virtually unknown today. It shows a box-cart, laden with *vraic* and drawn by two horses, ascending the slipway at Saline Bay, between Cobo and Grandes Rocques. The horses are wearing their 'winter clothes', for seaweed was normally gathered during that season. It was chiefly used as a fertiliser and this load was probably bound for a Castel farm. Nowadays, a box-cart is a museum-piece and horses are no longer used for haulage.

40. It has always been a common right for a Guernseyman to gather seaweed, or *vraic*. Each farm usually had its own *sécage* or drying ground on the coast. With the introduction of artificial manure, the practice of gathering seaweed from the shore has become almost obsolete. L'Erée, St Pierre du Bois, was one of the last places where the seaweed burners could be seen using a *sécage*. This photograph was taken in the 1960s.

41. Petit Bôt is one of the prettiest areas in Guernsey. Tw[...]
ancient watermills were situated here, fed by streams from
two nearby valleys. In 1827 the lower mill, now a tea-roo[...]
was used to make paper. One local newspaper, *L'Indépenden[...]*
was printed on paper produced there. Both mills ground co[...]
brought from the St Martin's side, as there was no road o[...]
the Forest side until after 1787. In about 1920, an hotel w[...]
built near the 18th-century tower but was destroyed by fir[...]
in 1940. The lower mill was also partly destroyed by the
Germans in 1944, as a reprisal after a British commando ra[...]
The upper mill (remains of which can still be seen) was al[...]
demolished for no other apparent reason than the fact tha[...]
foreign workers, employed by the German Organisation
Todt, were ordered to do so.

42. This sketch, by the late Charles Toms, depicts a cottag[...]
at Le Variouf, a charming settlement in the Forest parish
between Petit Bôt valley and Le Gouffre. Outside is a prar[...]
and stone steps lead to the arched doorway. The roof
comprises tiles and slates, with a skylight above a ground-
floor window. Happily, the charm of Le Variouf has surviv[...]
and this 1938 scene can still be enjoyed today.

43. In the early 1950s the Moulinet rock beacon off Castle Cornet needed repair. One characteristic of this sea-mark had been a bird carved from wood, which stood on the top of the beacon. The bird vanished during the war and, as a substitute, a wrought-iron bird was made by the States Works Department. Soon after it had been put into position, it was visited by sea-borne vandals and has never been seen since.

44. Le Souffleur, Torteval. When the wind is in the right direction this blow-hole near Baie de la Forge will send up plumes of spray – a most impressive sight. This photograph shows members of La Société Guernesiaise visiting the spot in 1962.

45. While the tomato industry in Guernsey is still important, it has declined somewhat since this photograph was taken some thirty years ago. The method of growing tomatoes has changed, as have the glasshouses. This photograph shows a particularly healthy crop, picked by hand and placed in baskets no longer used today.

6. The spectacle of a team of working horses ploughing a field in winter has vanished from our landscape. This photograph, taken in about 1953, is a reminder that this was just one of the many activities in which horses were once engaged throughout the farming year. Driving the team in the picture is Sam Allett who keeps a herd of dairy cows at Cleveland Farm, Rue des Crabbes, St Saviour's. His father, the late Alf Allett, would not countenance the use of tractors and continued to use horses throughout his life. In earlier years, the Alletts farmed at Les Grands Courtils, Grande Rue, St Saviour's. They grew a variety of crops including mangels, parsnips, carrots, kale, hay and potatoes. In those days only eight or nine cows were kept, compared with more than thirty nowadays.

47. & 48.   For more than 150 years, Le Hechet
Mill, St Martin's, was a conspicuous landmark.
It was built in the days when much corn was
grown on the island and several windmills were
erected in various parts of Guernsey. Le Hechet
had as its neighbour Les Vardes windmill,
St Peter Port, standing on the opposite side of
Les Ruettes Brayes. When Le Hechet Mill fell
into disuse it gradually became ruinous and
plate 47 (*above*) shows its condition in 1966. Soon
afterwards, it was excellently restored (*left*) and
was completely refurbished by 1967.

49. Heaps of rubble was all that was left of buildings on Lihou Island when the Woottons took it over in 1961. In the 19th century the tenants of the former farmhouse produced iodine from seaweed. The island has a desolate beauty which, in the 12th century, drew Benedictine monks to its shores. The remains of their priory still stand. The island is now inhabited by the Hon. Robin Borwick and his wife Patricia, who took it over at the end of 1983.

50. Colonel and Mrs. Patrick Wootton with two of their children on Lihou Island, where they set up home in 1961 and remained for a further 20 years. The former farmhouse and outbuildings were in a ruinous state when they rented the island, having been used for target practice by the German forces when they occupied Guernsey between 1940-45. After first removing 56 live shells whilst digging foundations, they built a workshop and then a six-bedroomed stone house. For 16 years, Colonel Wootton ran the Lihou Island Youth Fellowship and summer camps to give young people a 'constructive pattern for living'.

51. The ruins of the priory on Lihou Island as they appeared early in the present century. In the distance stands the 'Upper House', derelict and no longer used as a temporary watch-house, a role it filled when the French contemplated invading the Channel Islands. This building was destroyed by the Germans who, happily, spared the priory, although the dwelling house on the island was used as a target for German artillery on Guernsey's west coast.

52. During the German Occupation, anyone with either a sketch pad or a camera in evidence would have been picked up as a spy immediately. Charles Henry Toms, father of one of the authors of this book, was one of two appointed photographers whose task it was to photograph each member of the population for the purpose of issuing identity cards. Charles Toms, however, also made sketches on more than one occasion. This view is of the 16th-century house Les Blanches at St Martin's (the first and only house with an arch, on the right-hand side of Route des Blanches, travelling in the direction of Jerbourg). It shows a typically rural scene at St Martin's which, unfortunately, has vanished today. When this house was marked on the Duke of Richmond's survey of 1787 it was an isolated farm.

3. Le Guet, Cobo, as it looked about eighty years ago. The road, often so busy today, is empty, although horse tracks can be seen in the foreground. On the left of the ladies is the *Cobo Hotel.*

4. One of the most striking views inland from Vazon Bay is of La Grande Mare Country Club, which overlooks the broad acres of La Grande Mare itself. The complex of buildings partly occupies the site of the original Grande Mare House, seen in this pre-war photograph. It was once a farm, but in the 1930s it became a small hotel. It was a typical Guernsey country house which, like several others, lost its charm during the German Occupation. After the war, it was demolished and replaced by a far grander establishment.

55. Beaucette Quarry, near Fort Doyle, as it appeared whilst in use in 1935. A gun battery stood above it and helped to defend this part of Le Clos du Valle against a possible French invasion. The quarry was worked for many years but, soon after this photograph was taken, it became redundant and gradually filled with water. In 1967 it became the first Channel Islands' yacht marina. Royal Engineers blasted an opening on its seaward side, treating the operation as a training exercise. The quarry walls are well above sea level and the enclosed area makes an ideal marina.

56. A timber-built windmill, which once stood on the quarry edge, used to pump water from its floor.

7. Bordeaux Quarry was one of Guernsey's most important refuse dumps. It was one of the largest quarries on the island and was situated conveniently close to St Sampson's harbour, from where countless tons of its granite were exported until about 1950. This photograph, taken about fifty years ago, shows the quarry floor and lines along which horse-drawn trucks hauled the stone to a place where it could be hoisted to the surface. This was done either by a 'Blondin' cableway or by a steam crane, as in this photograph. The vast amount of spoil excavated from the quarry was used to form the foreshore of nearby Les Petils Bay.

8. A cottage at Le Bigard in the Forest parish, standing inland from La Corbière point. The cottage in the foreground is particularly attractive. Built of stone, it had a tiled roof, rising slightly on the left to permit an extra window to be added. This photograph, taken in the early spring of 1935, reveals countryside which has sadly lost some of its beauty over the years.

59. & 60. A windmill has stood on La Ville ès Pies (the place of the magpies) for two centuries and plate 59 (*above*) shows Vale Mill in its prime. This was when Guernsey grew wheat and the fields of Le Clos du Valle supplied much of it to what used to be called 'Hocart's Mill'. During the Occupation, the Germans used it as an observation post and increased its height, although they replaced the old mill cap on the top. Plate 60 (*right*) shows the mill after the Occupation. Since then it has been shortened somewhat. Although unsightly today, it continues to be a sea-mark for mariners, as it used to be in the days of sail.

Le Grantez Mill, seen here as a ruin in 1936, a victim of the German Occupation when a defence work was built on its site. It was one of several mills on Guernsey, most of which were built in the early 19th century at a time when much corn was grown on the island. This fine granite structure stood in the heart of our farming countryside but, together with most other Guernsey mills, it stopped working at the turn of this century and was allowed to fall into disrepair. The site of the mill tower still survives on the hilltop above the King's Mills.

62. Les Tielles watch-house, photographed in a ruinous state in 1938. It was one of a series of look-out posts around the coast, built at a time when invasion by the French was distinctly possible. It resembled its fellow at Mont Herault, not far from Pleinmont Point, which is still standing. The watch-house on the Torteval cliffs fell into ruins and what remained of it was destroyed when the Germans built a fortification on its site. Fortunately, the battery below remains intact and it was from this fine viewpoint that the photograph was taken.

Transport

63.   This photograph, taken in about 1910, depicts the days when visitors to Guernsey toured the island in four-in-hand excursion cars. It shows several such vehicles taking on passengers outside the *Royal Hotel*. Evidently, there was no lack of business and these 'cars' were invariably well-patronised. From their perches, passengers could see much of the countryside and the routes taken were often very attractive. Notice, on the left, the stately figure of the hotel porter.

64.   A box-cart and team photographed in the 1930s when such vehicles were commonplace. Today, however, they are museum pieces and draught horses can only be seen at island shows. At the time of this photograph, horse-drawn vehicles of this type were used to haul stone from the quarry to the stone-crushing mill at St Sampson's; they were also used to carry granite from the mill to ships. Box-carts were employed in carrying *vraic* from beach to farmyard, although long-carts (open-ended box-carts) were also used for this purpose. The box-carts were built locally of heavy timber as they needed to carry large loads. They were usually drawn by Shire horses and these looked especially attractive when, as in this photograph, they were resplendent with brasses.

65.   One of the last horse-drawn carts to be seen regularly in St Peter Port was owned by Walter Charles A. Watson of Les Cornus, St Martin's. He was 74 years old when this photograph was taken in 1961. His cart used to carry many goods including furniture, as well as taking tomatoes from vineries to the harbour for shipment to the U.K. During the 1950s 'Prince' (seen here taking a drink from a horse trough in Trinity Square) took his owner to town with the cart three times a week in summer and weekly in winter, to fetch the coal and do the shopping.

66. The first motor hearse arrived in Guernsey on 6 May 1928. The owner was James W. Way of Way's Garage, Pollet and Truchot. His father, Joseph G. Way imported the first motor cycle into Guernsey in 1899. The new hearse was a Buick master chassis of 27 h.p., with a London coach-built body and guaranteed four m.p.h. in top gear. This proved invaluable on 'walking funerals' when the hearse was followed by the mourners on foot. Christened 'Ursula', there was a mystery as to how the vehicle continued in use during the Occupation, when petrol had to be smuggled into the garage Ursula continued to run until 12 Februa 1943, when the fuel finally ran out and both Mr. and Mrs. Way were deported to a German internment camp at Laufen. Ursula survived the war but became obsolete in 1957 when she carried out her last journey to Le Foulon cemetery.

67. In the autumn of 1919 Stanley A. Noel left the Royal Flying Corps and started a garage business in Trinity Square at premises modestly called the 'Motor Engineering Depot'. He was in partnership with Cecil W. Noel, his brother, and Pat Greville. The firm were agents for Whitlock Motors. They also dealt in stove-enamelled cycle frames and imported one for Bucktrout and Co., wine and spirit merchants. This photograph shows the chassis of a Rio Speed Wagon at the depot. In the driving seat is Mr. Le Tissier (who later left to start Grandes Rocques Motors) with Alf Tostevin, Arthur A. Noel, –, and Stanley Noel. Bodies for this type of chassis were built by Wilf Le Huray at Ville-au-Roi coach works. These buildings were demolished in about 1937, to be replaced by St Peter Port Garages. This photograph was taken in 1925.

68. Mr. Alf Tostevin at the wheel of a Beeston Humber after it had been converted to a touring vehicle at the Motor Engineering Depot, Trinity Square, in about 1920.

69. A Rio Speed Wagon, one of the buses in the fleet of Bluebird vehicles owned by Falla Bros. in pre-war years. They operated between St Peter Port and L'Ancresse and the originals were Ford Ts. Bluebird buses were familiar sights for a great many years as they ran along Les Banques, across St Sampson's Bridge and then via Bordeaux to the L'Ancresse Terminus. Falla Bros. operated the service from 1925 until 1963, when their buses were sold to Guernsey Motors.

Kenneth Edward Bell

Kenneth Bell's tragic death, together with his wife, in a fire on the cruise liner *Lakonia* off Portugal in 1963, brought to an end a life of intense activity. Mr. Bell, of St Jacques, St Peter Port, started his working life as a motor cycle and motor mechanic at Millard's, who were then in Bosq Lane. He was later employed by a number of well-known island motor engineering firms. He became works manager of Bougourd Bros., Les Banques and was also local agent for the R.A.C., as well as being an insurance assessor. A very keen boatman, he owned a number of vessels. During the First World War, he joined the Royal Guernsey Light Infantry and went to France as a despatch rider. Between the wars he lived through the heyday of inter-island swimming and was among the band of enthusiasts who helped long distance swimmers achieve their goals by accompanying them in small boats. During the Occupation he managed Bougourd Bros. and, just 14 days after the Germans' arrival, he was

70. As a soldier in the Royal Guernsey Light Infantry, Ken Bell served in France as a despatch rider. He is seen here astride a Douglas motor cycle combination.

given charge of Motor House premises in The Avenue. Hidden away in the loft of Motor House was a small aircraft owned by Mr. Harold Le Parmentier. The Avro Avian had been taken there from L'Erée aerodrome before the war after sustaining damage. In 1940 it was in full state of repair except for the canvas cover and rudder. The loft door had been locked and the key taken by an employee.

In 1941 the Germans ordered that all inflammable materials be removed from the top stories of buildings. After considering the matter, Mr. Bell 'declared' the machine to the Germans. Unknown to him the machine was in full working order and freshly oiled. The suspicious Germans immediately took over the premises and placed an armed guard on the little plane. They then carried out an intensive investigation and Ken Bell was taken to Fort George and placed in solitary confinement for nine days with no exercise and little food. No charges were preferred against him and he was finally taken home by a Gestapo agent. The plane was removed to the airport and later taken to the harbour to be shipped to the continent. The owner, Mr. Le Parmentier, received no compensation whatsoever for his loss from the States of Guernsey after the war. At that time the aircraft would have been worth about £1,800.

71. Motor House, the garage in St Julian's Avenue (now the Royal Bank of Canada) in the loft of which the Avro Avian aircraft was hidden, in 1940.

72. The Avro Avian biplane at L'Erée aerodrome in 1936.

Since as long ago as 1917, islanders have been accustomed to the sight of aircraft in operation, for in that year a French flying boat base was established on the site of the temporarily demolished Model Yacht Pond. These small aircraft were transferred from land to water by crane, before taxiing out of St Peter Port. The base was closed down at the end of World War I.

In 1923 a flying boat service began operating between Southampton and Guernsey, run by the British Marine Air Navigation Co. Ltd. and later by Imperial Airways. Amphibian biplanes were used and the service continued until about 1930. In 1934 Guernsey Airways Ltd. was formed and De Havilland Dragons were employed. Our so-called airport was then at L'Erée and it was from there that Cecil Noel, the celebrated Guernsey airman, piloted the first Guernsey-built machine, the 'Wee Mite', in 1933. This area, however, was far from ideal and other sites were considered. Ultimately the fields at La Villiaze, Forest, were chosen by the States. They were 330 feet above sea level and comprised 130 acres, with a grass surface and a 3150 ft. runway. The 'aerodrome' cost £114,500.

73. The Imperial Airways amphibian *Calcutta* at its mooring in St Peter Port harbour. This three-engined flying boat operated between Southampton and Guernsey in the 1920s.

74. During the 1930s, R.A.F. flying boats sometimes visited Guernsey. In this photograph, three boats can be seen moored in the pool of St Peter Port, with the newly-constructed jetty behind them. They were very similar in appearance to the French aircraft of 1917.

75. In the summer of 1954, an R.A.F. Sunderland flying boat was about to taxi into St Peter Port when it hit an obstruction and only just succeeded in entering the harbour. Launches rushed to its assistance and towed the sinking aircraft to the careening hard, where it was beached above high water mark. There were no casualties, but the flying boat was eventually scrapped, although not before the public had inspected this unusual visitor.

76. La Villiaze terminal building under construction early in 1939. Over 130,000 cubic yards of soil were removed before surfacing and building could start and about seven miles of hedges had to be demolished.

77. La Villiaze airport was opened with great ceremony by the Secretary of State for Air, Sir Kingsley Wood, on 5 May 1939. He is seen holding the halyard which 'broke' the R.A.F. ensign on the roof of the terminal building, thus signalling the official opening. Four months later, war broke out and the airport was closed to civilians.

8. Among the deals in which Mr. Stanley A. Noel became involved was the purchase of Sarre Transport, which Stanley A. Noel Ltd. owned completely in 1947. The bus service, consisting of 23 buses, was established in 1924 by Mr. C. Le Gallez, when it was known as the Wayfarer Bus Service. It passed to Mr. Ernest Rugg, who later handed it over to his brother, William. Mr. Noel became a major shareholder in about 1951 and sold out to Guernsey Motors and the Guernsey Railway Company. He retired in 1967, having been island golf champion in 1934 and won nearly all the Open Competitions at one time or another. He played football for the Northerners F.C. from 1914 to 1929 and represented Guernsey in the Muratti Cup on eight occasions.

9. This rare photograph of a German steam train, running along a track between Bulwer Avenue and Longue Hougue Lane, was taken from a house named 'Brackenrigg'. This was one of several narrow gauge lines crossing, at that time, mainly open ground. In the distance can be seen three prominent buildings: Shotley Villa, Feldspar and St Sampson's church school. The area was virtually a marshalling yard for war materials entering the island. The tracks were of varying gauges and the train transported war materials from St Peter Port, northwards as far as the Vale Castle, westwards to Sandy Hook and south-westwards to L'Erée. This was a total of some 14 miles of 90-cm. railway. Frank E. Wilson, in his booklet *Railways in Guernsey*, wrote that lines were unfenced and ran along footpaths, drives, roadways, across fields and private gardens.

People

80.   Jean Breton's cottage as it appeared when he resided there. During the 19th century the cottage was altered substantially. It stands at Les Jenemies, St Saviour's, close to the west coast and was at one time visible from the sea. In June 1794 Captain Sir James Saumarez took a squadron of men-of-war from Plymouth to Guernsey and before sailing he met Breton at the Devon port. When the pilot asked Saumarez if he could be 'given a lift home', his request was readily granted. As the squadron sailed past Guernsey's west coast, a superior French fleet appeared and Saumarez resolved to take avoiding action. It was thanks to Jean Breton's local knowledge that the Royal Navy's vessels escaped to the safety of St Peter Port's roadstead. During one part of the operation, Saumarez asked the pilot if he was sure of his marks. 'Yes', replied Breton, 'for there is your house and there is mine'. He was referring to the mansion at Saumarez Park and his own humble abode.

1. (*above left*) Major-General Sir Isaac Brock was one of Guernsey's most illustrious sons. He was born in 1769 and spent his boyhood in a house in the High Street (now Boots the Chemists), which is commemorated with a plaque. At the age of 15 he joined the army and was appointed ensign in the 8th Regiment of Foot (the King's). By the age of 28, he was a Lieut.-Col. and in 1802, when he commanded the 49th Regiment, he was sent to Canada after the United States had declared war on Britain. By 1808 Brock was a Brigadier-General and three years later was promoted to Major-General. In 1811 he was made President and Administrator of the Government of Upper Canada and was knighted in 1812. In the same year, Canada was invaded by the Americans and in October, whilst he was commanding his troops on Queenston Heights, Brock was shot and died instantly. He was buried at Fort George (Canada) and an obelisk was erected in his memory on Queenston Heights. Brock University at St Catherine's, Ontario, was named in his honour.

2. (*above right*) Thomas De La Rue (1793-1866) founded the great firm which prints bank notes, postage stamps, playing cards and books, of worldwide repute today. He was born at Le Bourg, Forest, and when he was ten he was apprenticed to Guernsey printer and publisher Joseph Chevalier. In 1812 Thomas became editor of *Le Publiciste*, an island newspaper. A year later he started his own paper, *Le Miroir Politique*, later publishing *La Liturgie* with steel engravings. In 1816, seeking to better himself, De La Rue went to England where he made his fortune. After his death, his son, Warren, became head of the firm. In 1963 it printed *The Guernsey Farmhouse* for the Guernsey Society.

3. (*right*) George Le Boutillier, a Jerseyman, came to Guernsey when he was 21 and set up business as a draper in 1804. He had been educated at Elizabeth College and was one of those responsible for its reconstitution in 1826. His chief claim to fame, however, was the creation of the Commercial Arcade with his brother James. A vast amount of cliff-face was excavated and removed before work started on Guernsey's first pedestrian precinct but the project became so costly that the original idea of roofing the arcade had to be abandoned. The Le Boutilliers were ruined as a result of this enterprise and emigrated to America, where they did much better for themselves. Work on the arcade began in 1830 and was finished in 1838.

84. Marianne Miller (née Carey), the foundress of St Matthew's church, Cobo, in the last century. As a child she spent her annual summer holiday at Cobo and noticed that the fisherfolk living there had no church, so she persuaded her father, Charles Carey, to make enquiries as to whether one could be built. Eventually her plea was granted and sufficient funds were raised to pay for its construction. The girl's parents and her sister both subscribed £200 and other members of the family were equally generous. The church commissioners gave permission for the church to be built near Le Guet and it was consecrated by the Bishop of Mauritius on 6 December 1854. The site was donated by a Mr. de Beauchamp and the churchyard was the gift of the Revd. Lord de Saumarez and Col. the Hon. St Vincent Saumarez.

85. The Very Revd. Carey Brock, M.A., was born in 1825 and became rector of St Pierre du Bois in 1850. Later he was appointed Dean of Guernsey and he died in 1892. He was one of three consecutive rectors of the parish of the same name, the first being the Revd. Thomas Brock, who was rector in 1803 and died in 1850. He was succeeded by his son, Carey, who, in turn, was replaced by his son, Henry Walter, who became rector in 1892 and died in 1918. Of the three, the most outstanding was Thomas, who fiercely opposed those parishioners who forsook the church in favour of Methodism. Dean Brock was the first to conduct services in English, rather than French, in this country parish church.

86.   The premises of Le Lièvre Ltd. in Church Square are both attractive in their wares and historic in their siting, since they stand in one of the oldest parts of St Peter Port. The business was started in Guernsey in 1920 by Harold Francis Le Lièvre of Jersey and this photograph of his family was kindly loaned by the present head of the firm, Cyril Le Lièvre. From left to right are: Thomas Francis (father), Elsie, Harold Francis, his mother, Cyril Godfrey and (front) Clarence and Stanley. The photograph was taken in about 1900.

87. One of the customers F. H. Blicq's hairdressing establishment at no. 1, Hauteville was Victor Hugo who lived further up the street at Hauteville House during his exile on the island between 1856 and 1870.

88. The tinsmith's art has become a rarity in Guernsey and this photograph of William Richard James and his assistant recalls the time when such a business was not uncommon. Mr. James's shop was at no. 11, Bordage, almost opposite Tower Hill steps. He was also a coppersmith and specimens of his wares are well displayed in the window. He was in business during World War I and for a while afterwards, until Tudor House was built on the site of his shop.

89.   R. J. Collins and Co. were agents for Barratts, 'the great novelty confectionery' people. This specially constructed horse-drawn vehicle was seen on island roads in 1900. It had glass sides and was virtually a mobile shop. In the photograph are (*from left to right*): Stan Collins, R. J. Collins, Cliff Collins, W. Baudains and Percy Collins.

90.   After 95 years in the business of making Guernsey sweets, R. J. Collins and Co., established in 1879, ceased business in 1974. When Robert John Collins came to Guernsey, he was foreman sugar boiler at Keiler's sweet factory in Rue du Pré, now an office block. Keiler's moved to the Lower Pollet (opposite the *Thomas de la Rue* public house) and, when the firm left the island, Mr. Collins bought some of the machinery and set up his own sweet-making business. It was here that he met his wife, Miss Eliza Harriet Wilcox, who was forewoman over the lady packers. Mr. and Mrs. Collins moved their business to no. 9 Pollet, where the factory overlooked the harbour. In 1910 the firm acquired the property opposite, nos. 4 and 6, which were subsequently demolished and rebuilt. This picture shows a consignment of imported confectionery in the street outside no. 9. From left to right are: Sid Collins, R. J. Collins, Stewart Collins, − .

. After being in the Cumber family for 144 years, the old established pharmacy at no. 3 Le Pollet closed its doors for
e last time in 1962. It was founded by Mr. H. Cumber who came from England. As well as being a chemist, he also drew
eth. He was succeeded by his son, Henry J. Cumber, a prominent Quaker who took over the business in 1912. At the
ne it was probably the only shop in town without a telephone. It exhibited handsomely-coloured carboys and these still
.d the fish-tailed gas burners which once shed coloured lights into the street.

. In about 1897, Thomas Millard had a motor engineering business in Trowbridge, Wiltshire, where he advertised
me day repairs'. He came to Guernsey in 1908. In 1909 he set himself up at Bosq Lane, St Peter Port, where he
tablished a motor engineering business dealing in motor cycles and cars. The photograph shows Mr. Millard proudly
splaying an early motor cycle in the centre of Glategny Esplanade, with horse-drawn vehicles and a tram in the distance
ar the Salerie corner. In the 1920s, the business moved to Victoria Road, where Millard and Co. Ltd. is still going strong
nos. 9 and 11, after 60 years in the trade.

93. The time when hundreds of sheep roamed L'Ancresse Common is recalled by this picture which shows members of the Le Page family. Mrs. Sophie Le Page, in the centre holding a book, was for many years the shepherdess who watched over the flocks for various owners. She had 22 children, of whom 19 survived. When she was 94, in 1938, she was interviewed by the *Guernsey Evening Press*. Her husband, John Nicholas Le Page (*front row, second from left*), died in 1908. She then lived with her son-in-law and daughter, Pilot and Mrs. George Corbet at La Moye. She had a small white dog called Spot who rounded up the sheep for her. In the evenings as many as 200 animals would be seen wending their way near The Hermitage to enter the fold at La Pontière. Mrs. G. Corbet (*top row, second from left*) used to shear sheep for 3d. per head and knitted her own stockings from the wool, which cost 1s. per pound during the First World War. A single shearing might produce 7s. worth of wool. As for Guernsey mutton, a good fat sheep would fetch as much as £1. When Mrs. Le Page gave up as shepherdess, the job fell to one or more of her daughters and they continued until the gates, which kept the sheep from straying off the common, were removed. The photograph shows, from left to right: (*top row*) Bill Le Page, Mrs. G. Corbet, Mrs. Farley, George Le Page, Mrs. Ada Marquand, Mrs. Tom Ingrouille; (*front row*) Mrs. Lydie Plevin, John Nicholas Le Page (died 1908, aged 70), Mrs. Sophie Le Page (shepherdess), Mrs. Elsie Mahy, Mrs. Sophie Le Page (daughter-in-law) and Tom Le Page.

94. (*below*) Some of the Guernseymen who served with the 2nd Battalion of the Wiltshire Regiment, in Hong Kong between 1919 and 1921 and in India between 1921 and 1924. The photograph shows, from left to right: (*back row*) Dmr Jefferies, Ptes. Bayait, Druce, A. Pasquire, Hockaday, Boisell, Thomas; (*third row*) Pte. Bostrom, L/Cpl. Guilmoto, Pte. Hoare, Boy Brown, Ptes. Le Cras, Cleal, G. Le Roi, J. Le Roi, Gallie; (*second row*) Ptes. Le Prevost, Boalch, L/Cpls. Heaume, Marquand, Sgt. Phillips, Cpl. Rose, Ptes. Le Roi, W. Trump; (*bottom row*) Ptes. Druce, C. Couch, Ducellier, Lewis.

95. (*opposite above*) From 1900 to 1940 the Royal Guernsey Militia trained annually at Les Beaucamps. The militia came to an end just prior to the German Occupation and the huts are still remembered by many veterans. This photograph shows the picket, or guard, on duty on Sunday 10 September 1922: from left to right, (*back row*) Ptes. Le Page, Ozanne, White, Prout, Bourgaize, Queripel, Bailey, Envoldsen and Cochrane; (*middle row*) Pte. Bourgaize, L/Cpl. Machon, Cpl. Marsh, Sgt. Roberts, Cpl. Ingrouille, L/Cpl. Guille and Pte. de la Rue; (*front row*) Ptes. Blondel, Bailey, Knight, Rault, Allett and Cataroche. They were all members of No. 12 Platoon, 'C' company, 1st Battalion, Royal Guernsey Light Infantry.

96. (*below*) For almost five years, until the island's liberation in 1945, Guernsey's civilian population of over 23,000 struggled to survive. The States Essential Commodities Committee was responsible for ensuring the fairest possible distribution of available food, fuel, medical and other necessities. The committee faced a daunting task, not least with the transportation of food obtained from France, especially when control of the seaways fell into the hands of the Allies. On 7 August 1944, the island was finally besieged and no supplies got through until the day of liberation, 9 May 1945. From 14 February of that year until 7 March, there were no civilian bread rations; the Germans had requisitioned all wheat stocks. In a post-war report, the committee stated: 'The responsibility for the calamity and terrible suffering of being without bread was a state of affairs unprecedented in the known history of the island'. On 6 March, a consignment of flour and medical supplies was sent by the International Red Cross, but the general suffering and deprivation continued for a further two months. The Channel Islands were the last of the German occupied territories to be liberated. The photograph shows the staff of the States Committee for the Control of essential commodities, taken on 9 May 1945. From left to right: (*back row*) W. F. Druce, P. W. Le Ber, J. Mortie, F. A. P. Roberts, F. E. Edmonds, W. G. Le Page, H. Guilbert, K. Langlois, D. P. Honey, R. T. Martel, H. J. Mallett, U. H. Bisson, J. Baker, H. G. Till, E. C. Amy, H. Le Cheminant, J. Stevens; (*third row*) R. Bisson, E. F. Vaudin, K. L. Topp, A. de la M. Priaulx, D. Bynam, J. Adams, R. Lihou, H. V. Cleversley, J. F. Allen, M. O. Shirley, O. Le Page, K. E. Clark, D. Noakes, E. Wareham, M. M. Johns, K. V. Paine, W. M. Lane, A. F. Foster; (*second row*) A. T. Matthews, K. Langdon, K. Falla, R. Prevel, E. Ingrouille, – Turvey, I. Rose, F. E. Head, V. E. Carey, E. Bond, Z. Duquemin, E. Duquemin, M. O. Le Parmentier, E. C. Johns, I. Voute, M. M. E. Cherry, M. Symons, M. Rich; (*first row*) L. L. McKane, V. E. Luff, C. E. Gicquel, W. T. Wellington, W. D. M. Lovell, A. C. Richings, P. J. Le Maitre, J. H. Loveridge (secretary), Sir Abraham J. Laine, K.C.I.E. (president), Jurat P. de Putron, E. Stead, V. Creasey, C. de la Mare, J. P. Fustic, W. Bird, W. Tunbridge, G. P. Lowe.

97. The Castel Air Rifle Club, winners of the B.S.A. Cup, 1937-8: (*back row*) K. Martel, C. Le Jean, R. Archer (Hon. Sec.), L. Boucher, L. Rowe, C. Collins; (*front row*) A. Le Goff, T. Le Cheminant (president), J. Legg (captain), A. Archer (vice-president), S. Saltwell (coach).

98. A girls' class at the Castel school in 1937: (*back row*) D. Lock, R. Le Noury, Irene Steer, – Cluett, – Brehaut, D. Alles, Jean Blondel, –; (*centre*) Olive Bailey, Rita Collenette, Joyce Le Cheminant, Joyce Le Noury, Beatrice Le Prevost, Elsie Syvret, Christian Enevoldsen, Joan Guille, Doreen Le Cheminant; (*front*) Barbara Hudson, –, Vera Le Tissier, – O'Brien, Phyllis Trump, Ada Thoumine, Freda Dodd, Ivyna Ozanne.

). Edith Frances Carey was one of uernsey's greatest historians. Born in idia in 1864, she spent most of her life on e island where her family had long been tablished. Her girlhood home was Le allon, St Martin's, and throughout her 'e she made a study of local history and lklore. She edited Sir Edgar lacCulloch's celebrated *Guernsey Folk-e* and soon afterwards wrote *The Channel lands*, a handsome volume with ustrations by Henry Wimbush. She was erhaps the most outstanding member of a Société Guernesiaise, having been its esident twice and her contributions to s *Transactions* are of the utmost value to udents today. In 1927 she was elected Officer de l'Academie Française'. Some ars later she collaborated with her ousin Wilfred Carey in the sumptuous *istory of the Careys of Guernsey*. Following er death in 1935, La Société published *ssays in Guernsey History*, a selection of her apers previously unprinted.

100. One of Guernsey's most distinguished artists of modern times was William John Caparne, the recluse who lived in St Martin's from 1895 until his death in 1940. He moved from a house with a large vinery to the Bon Port cliffs, where he built a small bungalow standing in a sheltered garden. His studio was a disused tram car. There, living the simple life with his daughter, he concentrated on his painting. His work dealt chiefly with the magnificent cliff scenery of Guernsey, together with superb studies of its flowers. He was passionately interested in horticulture and was associated with the Royal Horticultural Society. Caparne was a modest, retiring man and the fine quality of his work was scarcely appreciated while he was alive, although it was not unknown on the island and, indeed, in the West Country. Nevertheless, during his long residence in Guernsey, his paintings became collectable, but it was only after his death, just prior to the Occupation, that they were appreciated to the full. Today his works fetch high prices.

101. Helen Wyatt (née Rowswell) was a familiar figure at the White Rock and New Jetty in pre-war days. She was invariably around when the mailsteamers docked, having walked from her home in Back Street. Helen sold fruit from the quayside to passengers on deck, using a shrimping net in which grapes or other produce were placed. She left the island upon the outbreak of the Second World War and never returned.

102. For many years, Miss A. Le Briseur kept an interesting public house at no. 12, Le Pollet, always known as 'Le Briseur's', adjoining what is now Gillow Furnishers' premises. The interior was unprepossessing; it was dark, rather uncomfortable and there were no adornments. Yet it was most popular among the business fraternity. It was said to be the only Guernsey pub without a name. This photograph shows the licensee in 1950, a year before her premises were sold for £5,200. Soon afterwards the building was demolished and became part of the furnishing business next door.

3.   When Bonnie Newton died in 1962, Guernsey
d Alderney were robbed of a remarkable character.
orn in Alderney in 1903, his mother kept the Victoria
arding house. John Lewis Newton went to sea school
the age of 12 and then went to sea. He returned to
s native island to become a fisherman. His boat, the
arie, was built in Alderney by Johnnie Beaucamp.
e came to Guernsey in about 1935 and in 1939 joined
e Royal Naval Reserve and soon found himself in the
dst of secret naval operations with the S.O.E. In
ptember 1942 he took part in a commando raid on
s Casquets lighthouse, in which the entire seven-
an garrison was captured. Under Major G. H.
arch-Phillips, Bonnie was the only member of the
rty of ten officers and two crew who knew intimately
e dangerous tides around these notorious rocks.
onnie took in the landing craft and also went ashore.
or his heroism and bravery during this and other
erations, he received the D.S.C. (for operations on
e French coast in 1942), the Croix de Guerre (for his
editerranean exploits) and the Croix de Guerre and
lm and Silver Star. He returned to Guernsey in 1945
d worked with L.C.T.s for two years. In 1947 he
arted the first Blue Arrow speedboat service to
erm. In about 1950 he bought the Brighton beach
at *Martha Gunn* and later the *Ben Gunn* to run
ssenger services to Herm and Jethou. His piratical
ture endeared him to his friends and customers who
ed to travel on the boats emblazoned with the skull
d crossbones.

104.   The youngest daughter of La Dame de Serk,
Jehanne Bell, was born in 1918 at La Vallette, Sark,
not long after the death of her father, Dudley
Beaumont. Her life was quiet, rather like her
personality, though there were outstanding moments.
One was in 1936 when she was presented to King
Edward VIII at a Buckingham Palace garden party.
Another was her election as a Deputy in Sark's Chief
Pleas. In 1947, she became engaged to Henry Parkin
Bell and in 1948 they were married. Jehanne was at
her mother's bedside when La Dame died in 1974 and
soon afterwards Mrs. Bell also lost her husband.
Jehanne Bell died in 1988, leaving many friends in
Sark, Guernsey and elsewhere.

105.   Frederick **H.** Best was born in Guernsey in 1905, one of a family of nine children, and was educated at Elizabeth College. For much of his life he worked at the meat market and farmed at Sunnyside Farm, Ruettes Brayes. Always interested in island affairs, 'Freddie' was elected a Deputy of the States, an office he held for several years. He died in 1974. He will long be remembered as a carriage driver when such vehicles had become rarities on the island. This photograph shows him driving his dogcart at Trinity Square; he often drove his family from their home to St Sampson's parish church, the horse and carriage being parked nearby until the service was over.

106.   When Helier Le Cheminant of Manila Cottage, St Pierre du Bois, was growing grapes under glass in the 1960s, the industry was dying. Scarcely more than one hundred tons were being exported from the island compared with 2,083 tons in 1913. The few grape growers left are in the south-west of the island and their fruit is sold on the roadside.

107. Guernsey's cooper at work at Les Vauxlaurens brewery. He was the late Mr. S. Clements who joined the firm of R. W. Randall Ltd. soon after the end of the last war. He retired in March 1970. His job was to make the casks and barrels in which beer was transported from brewery to pub. Randall's connection with Guernsey began in 1868, when R. H. Randall moved from Jersey to Guernsey and purchased what used to be called the Guernsey Brewery from Joseph Gullick in 1878. Gullick also owned a rope walk. The name was changed to Vauxlaurens Brewery and it is believed Mr. Randall purchased the wine and spirit business of W. Frecker at about that time.

108a. & b.   In 1941, during the Occupation, the Germans ordered that every adult in Guernsey and Sark be issued with identity cards. The task of photographing the adult population fell to two photographers: Charles H. Toms, of the *Guernsey Evening Press* Company, and A. J. Keates, a baker and confectioner, of Hauteville, St Peter Port. Plate 108a (*left*) shows Mr. Keates (on the left) and Mr. Toms waiting for 'customers' at their outdoor studio in Saumarez Park. Plate 108b (*below*) shows Mr. Toms photographing an islander at St Martin's, with Mr. Keates standing by. The auditorium at Candie Gardens and various glasshouses around the island were also used as studios.

109. The newspaper department of the *Guernsey Evening Press*, photographed in November 1942. From left to right, *standing*: S. O. Heaume, S. Vaudin, A. Guille, W. S. Udle, A. H. Ozard, S. Budge and H. Shayer; *sitting*: H. W. Bond, H. C. Hurrell, E. T. Le Page, C. H. Toms, J. E. Brett, C. E. Coker and C. E. Cluett.

"GENTLEMEN! THE SITUATION IS DESPERATE! WE ARE RUNNING OUT OF "ROAD CLOSED" SIGNS!"

110. The talented Guernsey artist Alan Guppy, who died in 1980, had a tremendous capacity to make people laugh whenever his drawings were published in the *Guernsey Evening Press* and *Star*. He had the knack of being able to distil humour from everyday local situations in such a gentle manner that he never caused offence. After selecting an idea, he would create an authentic background, aided by a camera, and produce splendid results. Many of his cartoons, like this one drawn in 1973, reflect the age in which we live.

Events

111.   To commemorate Queen Victoria's Diamond Jubilee in 1897, the people of Guernsey subscribed towards the cost of a statue of the queen which stands at the upper end of Candie Gardens. The pedestal, of Guernsey granite (quarried in the Vale parish and dressed at the yard of William Griffiths & Co. Ltd., North Side, Vale), was so massive that it required the power of a steam roller to haul it, on its heavy trolley, to its destination. The photograph shows pedestal and roller outside Griffith's yard, prior to the journey. The queen's effigy, in bronze, was designed by C. B. Birch, A.R.A., and is a copy of the one at Bombay, India. The figure is 8½ ft. high and the height of the entire pedestal is 10 ft. Three years after the Jubilee, on 1 March 1900, the statue was unveiled in heavy rain, similar to the weather conditions in 1863 when Prince Albert's statue was unveiled. At Candie Gardens, speeches were made by the Lieut. Governor and the Bailiff, in the presence of a fairly large crowd. There was indignation that the ceremony was held at such short notice, taking place on the day of the relief of Ladysmith during the Boer War, rather than on the Queen's birthday in May. The cost of the statue and pedestal was £700.

112. The choir of the Castel parish church, photographed by Thomas Bailey at Easter 1914, when the members were robed for the first time. The only robed members were men and boys; the ladies continued to wear their 'Sunday best'. At the time, the rector was the Revd. P. S. Mesny.

113. The induction of the Revd. Leslie Marcus Quehèn as rector of St Sampson's on 25 July 1916. The Bishop of Winchester stands facing the camera, with the young rector beside him. Other clergy, choristers and some of the congregation are grouped around the west door of the church, which is closed. Until the rector requested entry it would remain so – all part of the institution of a new incumbent.

114.   The royal visit of 1921, when King George V, Queen Mary and Princess Mary came to Guernsey in very hot weather. Here they are seen at Cambridge Park, accompanied by Sir Edward Ozanne, Bailiff (on the left), and Lady Ozanne (behind the Queen). Schoolchildren flanked the path, strewing flowers as the royal party advanced, smiling happily and watched by a great many spectators, some of them visible in the background. The heat was so intense that later in the day Her Majesty almost fainted.

15.   The choir of St Sampson's parish church, photographed between 1945 and 1950. In the centre is the Revd.
C. L. Frossard, who was rector from 1918 to 1965, Dean of Guernsey from 1947 to 1967 and later a canon of Winchester
Cathedral. He died in 1968. On the left of the middle row is churchwarden John Hamon, with his fellow warden, Stafford
Ogier, on the right. The women members are wearing mortar boards, which were discarded a few years later. The rector
is flanked by lay readers. The choir was far larger than it is at present.

16.   Members of the Old Elizabethan Association grouped outside Elizabeth College on the occasion of the 100th O.E.
dinner in 1985. This was held in the College Hall, the traditional venue for such functions, although occasionally St James'
Hall is used.

117.   On 29 June 1935 a fire broke out in what was formerly the premises of Lovell & Co. Ltd., Smith Street. Almost opposite was the Press Office and one can imagine the excitement there when the fire was noticed. Both a reporter and photographer were rushed to the scene and this picture was taken from an upper window of Boots' premises. In the foreground is the fire engine, 'Sarnia II', as well as numerous spectators. They appear to be only mildly interested in the firemen at work and it seems to have been more of a social occasion than a disaster. Doubtless the fire was not serious.

Harbours, Fishing & Shipping

118. This, surely, must be one of the oldest photographs of St Peter Port, dating as it does from about 1860, for it was not until 1862 that the castle breakwater was extended beyond the emplacement, on which the Model Yacht Pond was later built. In the foreground are barges used in the transport of stone from one site to another. The scene may have presented rather a desolate prospect, but this photograph is of definite historical value.

119. This photograph shows the rebuilding of the North (or Victoria) Pier more than a century ago. The foreground is roughly where the careening hard is now and sailing craft are secured along the pier. Clearly visible is the handsome lighthouse which once graced the South (or Albert) Pier. On its left is a stretch of rocky beach, later to be covered by the emplacement.

120. This photograph must date from about 1860, since it shows the rebuilding of the South Pier (now part of St Peter Port's marina) which took place between 1859 and 1862. Along the Quay are the premises of Grace & Son, sailmakers (now La Nautique restaurant), the *Vine Hotel* (now a sweet shop) and on the skyline is Marshall's Royal Yacht Club Hotel (now Boots the Chemists). Below was a billiards saloon (now the United Club), the *Crown Hotel* (now the *Ship and Crown*) and the plantation on which the States Office was built in 1911. Part of the North Pier can be seen and, on the right, stands an elegant lighthouse. It occupied the site of a small prison, in which felons awaited transportation by boat to the larger prison in Castle Cornet. This served as Guernsey's gaol until the States Prison was built in 1811. Unfortunately, the old lighthouse was later demolished and replaced by the less attractive Red Light.

1. This smart-looking steamer, the *Antelope*, was one of three packets owned by the Great Western Railway and employed on the Weymouth-Channel Islands route. They were built in 1889 and each had a gross tonnage of 596. Their speed was 16 knots. The *Antelope* was sold in 1913 and operated in Greek waters until she was broken up in 1933. In June 1890, the steamer became stranded on rocks off Herm, but a few hours later she was removed without any serious damage to her hull.

122. Berthed in the Old Harbour, where she discharged coal, is the Dorey steamer *Perelle*. A typical collier of the 1930s, she steamed from England or Wales to Guernsey with house coal or anthracite, along with several of her sisters in the Dorey fleet. It was usual for these ships to load stone from St Sampson's as they returned for more fuel for island fires.

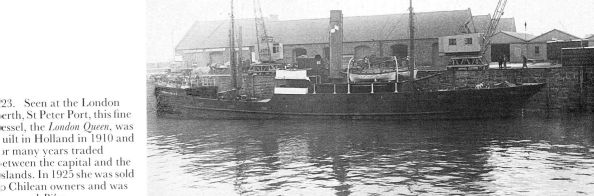

123. Seen at the London Berth, St Peter Port, this fine vessel, the *London Queen*, was built in Holland in 1910 and for many years traded between the capital and the islands. In 1925 she was sold to Chilean owners and was renamed *Pilar*.

124.   Berthed at the White Rock, perhaps eighty years ago, is a Great Western mail steamer, probably the *Reindeer*. She has arrived from Weymouth and is about to sail to Jersey. Horse-drawn vehicles await fares and several spectators are looking on. The ship was built in 1897 (like her sister, the *Roebuck*) and remained in service until 1928.

125.   St Peter Port's New Jetty was completed in 1928 and provided more accommodation for ships using the harbour. In this photograph can be seen the Weymouth mail steamer *Reindeer* (left), the Southampton-based cargo ships *Ulrica* and, berthed on her inner side, *Aldershot* (originally named *Brittany*). The Weymouth boat is seen approaching her berth, while the others are preparing to discharge their cargoes. The photograph dates from about 1925. Congestion such as this was eased with the completion of the jetty.

126. There has been a lifeboat stationed in Guernsey since 1803. The vessel in this picture was named *Queen Victoria* and was built in 1929. She was christened by Lord Ruthven, the island's yachting Lieutenant-Governor. She served Guernsey until 1955, except for the war period when she happened to be at Cowes, Isle of Wight, for overhaul, just as the island was being occupied by the Germans. During that period she served as a relief lifeboat at several English stations before being sent to Eire. She was replaced by the *Euphrosyne Kendal*, which has since been replaced by the modern Arun Class vessel, *Sir William Arnold*.

127. In 1967 a young couple enjoying the solitude of Saints fishermen's harbour on a balmy summer night were rudely disturbed by the arrival of a great ship. She was the *President Garcia*, with 9,500 tons of copra aboard, bound from Manila to Rotterdam and sadly off course. Miraculously, she missed several rocks in the bay before coming to rest a few yards from the astonished couple. There she remained for several days, a tremendous attraction to the local people until, on 20 July, she was towed away, stern first, to Rotterdam, where she was repaired.

128.   Until the outbreak of the Second World War, St Peter Port was regularly visited by lordly yachts of a tonnage almost unknown today. Several were palatial steam yachts, but there were plenty of sail-driven pleasure craft, usually with auxiliary engines. This photograph shows the tops'l schooner *Oceana*, berthed in what was then the Old Harbour, at the Red Light berth. She had been built in 1880 and the picture was taken in about 1935. Under sail she made a handsome sight which islanders often enjoyed. Today, vessels like these are rarities and the Old Harbour is now the Victoria marina.

29. In 1964, when divers discovered an easy way of harvesting crayfish from the sea, there was an outcry from traditional fishermen. Soon, however, the crayfish all but disappeared and these shellfish remain in very short supply.

30. Fishermen are no longer seen hawking fresh mackerel on the streets. One of the last was Fred Berryman who, during the mackerel season, was often seen at the bus station. He was a great character and an accomplished storyteller. He often made willow crab and lobster pots on the slipway at the Albert Pier. This picture was taken in 1965.

131. Queen scallops were found in large quantities by fishermen trawling on banks south of Sark in the early 1970s. The bonanza was short-lived, however. This photograph shows a net full of queens, on board the trawler *Hopeful Venture*, owned by Frank Le Page.

132. Taking seaweed from North Beach, St Peter Port, for use on the land in December 1953. Thirty years after this photograph was taken, the States voted £9,866,000 for the first phase of a new development to create a car park for some 800 vehicles and a 20-acre marina for 670 yachts by filling in this beach.

133. This handsome lighthouse, standing at the end of the castle breakwater, was designed by the celebrated Guernsey artist, Peter Le Lièvre and shone for the first time in 1867. Its fellow, across the pierheads on the Spur, was also designed by him. The breakwater light and that which shines from Belvedere, Fort George, form the leading lights which guide the mariner down the Little Russel and into St Peter Port. These lighthouses and the breakwater formed part of the so-called 'New Harbour' which was built between 1860 and 1880.

St Sampson's

134. From some unspecified time in the last century until the early years of the present one, St Sampson's parish church was covered with ivy. Doubtless it made a pretty sight, but the plant was injurious to its ancient masonry and the ivy was eventually removed, leaving the old stone visible again. This photograph was published in postcard form. Its caption unfortunately stated that the church was built in 1111 though, in fact, it was probably much earlier.

. In 1919 a serious landslide occurred at Longue Hougue
rry, St Sampson's, the property of A. & F. Manuelle Ltd.
re was a fall of 12,000 tons of stone and rubble and a woman
her life as a consequence. She was feeding rabbits in one of
houses seen above the landslide when she and her pets were
pt to their death. At about the same time a dolmen was
covered nearby in Delancey Park and there were those who
eved that the rifling of this prehistoric tomb was somehow
ponsible for the quarry tragedy. It must be admitted that
lier interference with prehistoric remains resulted in loss of
to those living in the vicinity. A far more serious landslide
urred at this quarry in 1969 when much of the nearby
veyard was swept into the quarry, carrying with it human
nains. As a result, work at the Longue Hougue was
ndoned and today the quarry has become a reservoir.

Landslide at a St. Sampson's Quarry, Guernsey.
(Fall of 12,000 tons, resulting in loss of life)
Bramley's Topical Photos, St. Julian's Avenue

5. Stonecrackers at work near Mont Crevelt, close to Longue
arry, in the early years of this century. This hard labour was
carried out in the Guernsey prison.

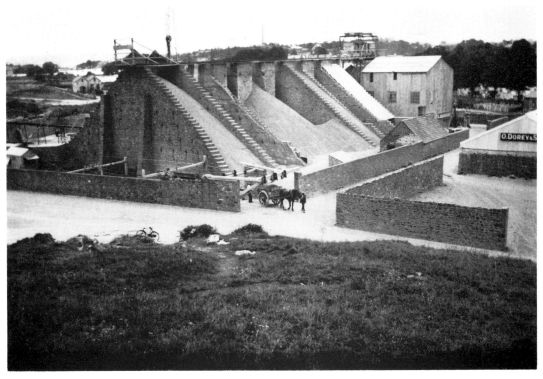

137.   The crushing plant of A. & F. Manuelle Ltd., adjoining their Longue Hougue quarry, as it appeared in 1938. The photograph, taken from Mont Crevelt, shows a horse-drawn box-cart leaving the crushers and the various grades of stone can be seen in the background. The plant hides the top of the quarry, which ceased operations in 1969.

138.   In 1963 the *English and Guernsey Arms* at South Side, St Sampson's, closed down and moved to more spacious premises nearby. One of the oldest public houses on the island, it was established in the 1880s. A fire damaged the original premises and the house in the picture was rebuilt in 1933. Its most recent role was that of a car showroom.

139. Le Crocq, on the south side of St Sampson's harbour, as it appeared in the heyday of the granite industry. This emplacement was built in 1864, when the harbour was extended to cope with the amount of stone being exported. It reached its zenith just before the outbreak of the First World War, which was probably when this photograph was taken. Visible are several sailing vessels and two steamers, all of which would load stone for England, having brought coal to the island from South Wales and other parts of the United Kingdom for both domestic and commercial use, as much anthracite was needed for the growing of grapes and tomatoes. Typical local fishing craft appear in the foreground. Apart from the shipping, the scene today is much as it used to be 80 years ago, although now more ships are laid up there in the winter. Le Crocq has two memorials. One near the quayside, thought to be of prehistoric origin, commemorates Daniel de Lisle Brock (a former Bailiff), who favoured the harbour's improvement. It was set up in 1873. The other, obelisk-shaped and of the same date, recalls the States committee responsible for the same undertaking.

Alderney

140. The wreck of H.M.S. *Viper* off Alderney in August 1901. This destroyer, one of the fastest in the Royal Navy and newly built, was engaged on manoeuvres with the Channel Fleet when, in dense fog, she struck the Renonquet reef near Burhou at 22 knots. The impact ripped out her bottom and she became a total loss. No lives were lost, but the remains of the *Viper* were blown up, after her guns and torpedoes had been salvaged.

141.   This photograph, taken before the First World War, shows Harry Main outside his forge at Le Huret. An employee is shoeing a horse in the street, while two youngsters look on. This was a typical example of the quiet, informal and delightful atmosphere which prevailed in Alderney until 1940. Many horses used its roads, transporting agricultural produce and stone to the harbour, although a good deal of stone arrived from Mannez by rail. This old blacksmith's forge is no longer there, but the building still survives.

142.   Le Huret, Alderney, as it looked in about 1910. This corner of St Anne's remains attractive. The clock tower still stands beside the present Alderney Society's museum (then a school) and the other buildings are much as they used to be. Unfortunately, the gas street lamp no longer adorns the scene.

143.   Precisely why Victoria Street, Alderney, is beflagged is not apparent for this postcard, published by C. R. Le Cocq,
bears no caption. Perhaps it was in honour of the Duke of Connaught's visit in 1905. On the right stood the *Victoria Ho*
which today stands opposite, and a gift shop now occupies its original site. Superficially, this paved street looks much a
it did 80 years ago. A closer inspection today, however, reveals modern shopfronts and a lack of Alderney names over ther

144.   A pastoral scene in Alderney, photographed many years ago. It shows a corner of Rose Farm and on the back of the postcard is written 'Aunty Fanny's Farm'. The family (doubtless including Aunty Fanny) are seen with some of their animals and a corner of the farmhouse is also visible. Today Rose Farm continues to be important to the agriculture of the island and can be seen from the road leading past the airport westward.

145.   Water Mill Farm, at the foot of Le Petit Val, as it appeared before the First World War. The house was built in 1792. Water can be seen cascading over the wheel and some of the farm animals, including a fine pig, are also in the picture. The stream running down Bonne Terre fed the mill. Because the water supply proved to be insufficient, a reservoir and leat were built on the hillside overlooking Platte Saline and this is marked on James Wild's map of 1833. The actual mill has long been out of use, but the residence is still occupied. A document dating from 1236 reveals that Alderney was once divided into two equal parts, one the property of the Crown and the other belonging to the Bishop of Coutances, who possessed a water mill. Perhaps the mill in this picture was built on the site of the medieval mill.

146. Before the First World War there was a Lloyds Signal Station on Butes, the viewpoint near St Anne's, and the groove in this block of granite is believed to have been where the watchman rested his telescope, which was often trained on Les Casquets lighthouse. Although there is no longer a station here, the grooved stone serves as its memorial.

147. In the early 1920s, Alderney saw its first passenger transport and the first regular bus service was run by A Langlois of Newtown. For many years the Simon family operated a service and the photograph shows the 1933 'Eastern Belle' in action. After the German Occupation Alderney's bus service was resumed and the Simons oper it until 1987. It continues today under new ownership.

148. During the German Occupation the bells of St Ann church were taken to France, where it was planned to melt t down for ammunition. Happily this was done towards the end the Occupation and, soon after D-Day, allied troops discovere them near Cherbourg. They w eventually returned to Alderne and were temporarily hung fro frames in the churchyard. The l had been replaced by a Germa machine gun and observation and before they could be rehur much work had to be done to t vandalised church. The bells remained outside the west doo until 1953 when, from the belfr they rang out in honour of the Queen's Coronation. The photograph shows two of them their massive timber frames.

9. This Danish seine vessel, stranded on Braye beach, Alderney, was abandoned there during the German Occupation.
August 1948, the vessel was repaired and towed to Guernsey, but it is not known what happened to her subsequently.
s interesting to note that this old fishing craft was wrecked in the same gale which caused the SS *Staffa* to founder near
aye's inner harbour, in 1943.

150. Alderney pilot Sam Ingrouille is seen here at the tiller of his boat *Flapper* in pre-war days, when
the island had five working pilots. The Ingrouille family originated from Guernsey's Bordeaux area.
Sam and his brother Dan lived near their sister, Mrs. Mary Blestel, who drove a donkey and a trap,
selling fish on behalf of local fishermen. The *Flapper* appears to be taking visitors to Burhou.

151.   During the 1950s, attempts were made to establish new industries in Alderney. One of these was the meat processing factory at the Arsenal, below Fort Albert. This photograph shows great tubs of sausage meat being tipped into boxes, each of which held 56 lbs. These were then pushed onto the production roller line for final packing. Several men and women were so employed and for a time the business was successful. However, problems of transport arose and this was one of the reasons why the factory ultimately closed. Other enterprises of this period included the manufacture of car silencers at the Penguin Works, Newtown, and the growth of vast quantities of market garden produce on and around the Blaye. Again, the difficulty of shipping such products to England caused these industries to be abandoned.

152.   Until about 1960, Alderney boasted a town crier. This photograph shows Dick Haycock who was an old soldier, as was his bell, so to speak, for it bore the War Department's broad arrow on its side. The town crier would make announcements of local interest from various vantage points in St Anne's, notably at the top and foot of Victoria Street and in Marais and Royal Connaught Squares. Today, the custom has lapsed (save for a brief resurrection during Alderney Week) and local announcements, if any, are made from loud-speaker vehicles.

3. In 1960, W. Le Vallée's mineral water factory in Marais Square was turned into a garage. Ruette Braye Motors of ernsey opened the premises in May of that year and became a service depot and a petrol and oil station. Now called derney Motors, it is still very much in business.

4. In 1972 the granite crusher at Braye was finally removed. For years it had dominated the scene and, because it had en reinforced by the Germans during the Occupation, its demolition presented a problem. The work took a long time d, even today, some of its ugly concrete can be seen on the beaches adjoining the harbour. Equally unlovely was the esence of derelict cars at Braye, but fortunately they are no longer abandoned there.

155.   Second only to Fort Albert in size is Fort Tourgis, on the slopes overlooking the Swinge. At one time the Royal Alderney Militia used it, as did the Germans, but in post-war years it has been virtually abandoned and its present condition is grievous. For several years its only human occupant was Mrs. Jean Neish, who established a bird sanctuary within the walls of the fort. A *Guernsey Evening Press* reporter visited her in 1973 and found that her 'family' included a tame jackdaw, a dozen cats, three gulls, two Chinese geese, over one hundred pigeons and an Alsatian dog. Some of these creatures appear with Mrs. Neish in the photograph. Today Fort Tourgis is empty, for Mrs. Neish has left Alderney and her 'family' has long been dispersed.

Sark

156.   The schooner, *Cheval de Troie*, *c*.1880. This was the first coal vessel to go right into the Creux Harbour, Sark. The vessel was wrecked off Flamborough Head in November 1882, while on a voyage to Guernsey. Of the crew of six, only one man was saved. The paddle steamer is the *Rescue* (the second of that name), built in 1878.

157. The old tunnel at Creux Harbour, Sark, was built by Helier de Carteret, the first Seigneur, in 1588. This old photograph was taken from the landward entrance, in which a fishing boat and crabpots were stored. The seaward end is bathed in sunshine. During the Occupation the Germans filled the old tunnel with stones, leaving only the modern one in use. Today the old tunnel is only traversed by those bound for the beach in Creux Harbour.

158. In 1880, St Peter's church, Sark, was greatly enlarged by the addition of a chancel and this photograph shows the laying of its foundation stone. The chancel was the gift of the Seigneur, the Revd. W. T. Collings.

159. This photograph, taken on 3 July 1916, is a fine study of fashions in Sark and shows children and teachers from the Sunday school, who were doubtless about to enjoy their annual 'treat'. They are grouped outside a shop whose roof, like so many in the island, is of corrugated iron. The fact that everyone is wearing a hat is a sign of the times.

160.   La Coupée, Sark, links Big and Little Sark and without it there could be no communication between the two. From time to time, its surface requires attention, since the isthmus is of a friable nature. The photograph shows men repairing the road in April 1932. Work on the Jersey side must have been hazardous, since there is a sheer drop to the sea. The side above Grande Grève (on the left of the picture) is less steep. In the summer of 1945 La Coupée underwent a major operation, for during the German Occupation little attention was paid to its condition. A new surface and stouter railings were installed, chiefly by prisoner-of-war labour under the supervision of the Royal Engineers.

161.   In 1947, Lieut. Gen. Sir Philip Neame, V.C., was Guernsey's Lieut. Governor and that summer he visited Sark to present prizes at the island's cattle show. Here he is seen presenting one to La Dame de Serk, watched by her daughter, Mrs. H. P. Bell. On the right is Lady Neame.

162a. & b. The visit of Princess Elizabeth and the Duke of Edinburgh to Sark in the summer of 1949 was a great event, for until then royal visits there had been scarce. Plate 162a (*above*) shows the scene at La Maseline harbour, where the Princess and Duke landed from a motor torpedo boat; in plate 162b (*right*), the visitors are seen at the entrance to La Seigneurie with their hosts.

163. When Field Marshal Montgomery visited Sark in 1947 he lunched at La Seigneurie with Mr. and Mrs. R. W. Hathaway. Several photographs were taken of his visit and 'Monty' is seen here with the indoor staff of La Seigneurie.

164. In 1949 the then Home Secretary, Mr. Chuter Ede, paid Sark a visit and he is seen here with La Dame (Mrs. Sibyl Hathaway), inspecting the guard of honour furnished by the local branch of the British Legion, whose members proudly display their medals. Chuter Ede was deeply involved in reshaping the constitutions of Guernsey, Jersey and Alderney, although that of Sark remained substantially unaltered.

165a. & b.   In April 1951, Sark was the location for filming 'Appointment with Venus', in which the island figures prominently. The story deals with the German Occupation of the island, but in a light-hearted vein. Islanders were invited to act as extras. Plate 165a (*above*), shot at Creux harbour, shows a German soldier sternly regarding the islanders. Plate 165b (*below*), taken at the same spot, shows 'Germans' driving through the tunnel (appropriately adorned with their insignia) with the cow 'Venus' in the truck behind the tractor. The film was a great success, as was the novel of the same name by Gerard Tickell.

166.   A wedding in Sark is an event which almost the whole island celebrates. On 10 March 1949, Thomas Hamon was married to Henriette Hamon at St Peter's church. After the wedding, this photograph was taken at La Ville Farm. In the photograph are, from left to right: (*standing*) Roy Mann (bridegroom's nephew), Dora Hamon (bridegroom's sister-in-law), Don Guilliard (friend), Margaret Baker (bridesmaid and friend), Thomas Hamon (bridegroom), Henriette Hamon (bride), Isabel Baker (bridesmaid and friend), John Hamon (bridegroom's brother and best man), Louise and John Baker (friends); (*front row, seated*) Jane Hamon (bride's grandmother), Doris Mann (bridegroom's sister), Rosina Hamon (bridegroom's mother), Philip Hamon (bride's father), Henriette Hamon (bride's mother), Louise Carré (friend and grandmother to the two bridesmaids).

167.   A photograph of the funeral procession of Mr. William Carré of La Marguerite, Sark, who died in 1950. A much respected islander, he was a member of the local branch of the Royal British Legion and of the 'Buffaloes' Society. The banner of the legion heads the cortège and members of both organisations are seen bearing the coffin and carrying wreaths, as they proceed towards St Peter's church. As is customary in Sark, the coffin is borne by bearers, for there is no hearse on the island and such processions invariably make very impressive spectacles as they travel along Sark's quiet roads.

168.   The Island Stores, Sark, in 1959. On the left are the proprietors, Mr. and Mrs. Hubert Lanyon, with their family grouped behind the counter. This was a typical village store in the Avenue, which sold wares of all kinds, including bread and cakes from the bakery behind the shop. Hubert Lanyon, a Guernseyman, settled in Sark in 1928 and played a prominent part in the island's political, business and sporting activities.

169.   Denis John Le Goubin, together with his wife, started a bakery business in Sark in 1956 and this sturdy carrier cycle was used for deliveries. Cyclists still pay £1 a year in tax on their machines. Mr. Le Goubin made the silver wedding cake for La Dame de Serk (Mrs. S. M. Hathaway) and Mr. Hathaway, and also assisted with the catering for a garden party held in honour of Princess Margaret's visit to Sark in 1959.

70. During the German Occupation of Guernsey, the St John Ambulance Brigade was obliged to use a horse-drawn vehicle when petrol supplies were unobtainable for their motor ambulances. After the war the vehicle was surplus to requirements and Sark was only too willing to accept it. Here it is seen with the late John Perrée at the reins. It served its purpose in Sark for several years, but at last became unserviceable and is now on show at the German Occupation Museum in Guernsey. Its replacement in Sark is a tractor-drawn trailer ambulance.

71a. & b. To commemorate the 400th anniversary of the granting of the Royal Charter by Queen Elizabeth I to Sark in 1565, four medallions were struck, three in gold and one in silver. The arms of La Dame de Serk (Mrs. Sibyl Hathaway) are on the obverse (*below left*) and those of the first Seigneur, Hilaire de Carteret, are on the reverse (*below right*). At an anniversary party held in August 1965, island schoolchildren were each presented with a medal.

172. For many years the Falle family owned *Stock's Hotel*, Sark, and their launch, the *Sheila*, was often used to convey their guests to and from the island. The photograph shows Sheila Falle naming the boat, watched by her father, Bertie Falle, an island personality and great character. In the background are Pilot Philip Guille and Messrs. W. H. and Henry Carré. The launch was a former liner's lifeboat and could be seen at St Sampson's harbour until quite recently.

173. On 23 September 1960, Hubert Lanyon, one of Sar bakers, saw in the *Baker's Review* a reference to a loaf whic measured over five ft. in length. This was obviously a challenge and did not escape his attention. On the occasio of Sark's autumn produce show, he decided to make a loa which would certainly beat that length and perhaps establi a new record. The result was a loaf six ins. in diameter, eigh ft. long and weighing nine lbs. The monster loaf attracted widespread attention and after the show was put up for auction and raised 30 shillings. Highest bidder was Reube Martel of Guernsey, who strapped the loaf to a wooden plan and took it back to Guernsey on the launch *Highland Ladd* The loaf was again exhibited in the Guernsey market, where people were asked to give donations in aid of the island's effe for World Refugee Year. The photograph shows Mr. Marte (on the right) holding the loaf, assisted by Colin Hodgetts.

74.   The late Adolphus Hamon of Little Sark with his carriage. Known as a 'chair', it resembles a victoria except that it has doors. The padded section is hinged so that when passengers are seated, the section can be lowered for their protection against the elements. Sark's horse-drawn vehicles were, for the most part, built either in Guernsey or Jersey and many must be over 100 years old. They are maintained in first class order as replacements would be most expensive.

Herm

175. An early photograph of Herm showing the Mansion, farm buildings, cottages and, behind them, the former mill tower. Fields lie in the foreground and the walled gardens and woodlands adjoining the mansion are seen on the right. Just to the right of the tower is a building subsequently known as 'Lady Perry's House'. It recalls the time when Sir Percival Perry was Tenant of Herm, after Compton Mackenzie had forsaken the island in favour of Jethou. Sir Percival preferred to reside in what is now the *White House Hotel*.

176.   Seining for sand eels off Belvoir, Herm, in 1950. The *Mildred* was owned by the late Capt. H. Petit, seen in the centre of the group. His son, Capt. John Petit (on the left), was a former St Peter Port harbourmaster.

177.   The sand eels were kept in a *courge*, a wickerwork 'basket' pointed at both ends and usually towed behind a fishing boat on its way to the fishing ground. The fish – red and green – were used as bait for catching whiting, or on long lines for catching skate or other flat fish.

178.   A fine collection of Herm ferry boats, photographed in 1950. They were the *Capwood*, *Lady June*, *Arrowhead*, *Maywood* and *Martha Gunn*. In those days, all boats running to Herm were completely open. In bad weather, passengers were protected by tarpaulins.

9. The cargo/passenger boat *Celia* did valiant service between Guernsey, Herm and Sark from 1928 onwards. When ompton Mackenzie relinquished the lease of Herm from the Crown, it was taken over by Lord Perry, chairman of the rd Motor Corporation. He had the *Celia* specially built in Glasgow to carry cargo to Herm from Guernsey. She was 40 ft. 1g, 12 ft. 3 ins. in the beam and was skippered by 'old' Fred Zabiela whose son, 'young' Fred, took over after his father's ath. When Lord Perry left Herm at the outbreak of the last war, he left the vessel to his skipper. The *Celia* was fitted with 36 h.p. Kelvin Ricardo paraffin engine and was an excellent sea boat. The two Zabielas, father and son, were both eboatmen and were on the St Peter Port relief lifeboat when she was straffed by the Luftwaffe on 28 June 1940, whilst on ourney between Guernsey and Jersey. The coxswain, Harold Hobbs, was killed. The *Celia* was subsequently sold to the ood family of Herm and used as a cargo and passenger vessel until she was finally disposed of and sent to Jersey.

0. Herm's first school was established as long ago as 1838, when the Revd. Henry Benwall, aided financially by St Peter rt parishioners, sought to educate the children of the quarrymen working in Herm. However, the men saw no reason ny their children should be educated and, as they declined to make any contribution towards the cost, the school closed 1840, despite the fact that 40 children lived on the island. It was not until 1955 that another attempt at educating the ildren of Herm residents was made and this time it was a success, thanks to the support of the States Education Council. hildren are taught there until the age of 14 years, after which they receive further tuition in Guernsey. The photograph, ken in 1955, shows the schoolmistress, Mrs. Maureen Corboy, with some of her pupils. From left to right are: (*front row*) mon Wood, Martin Ray and Jo Wood; (*back row*) Susan Muttock, Jennie Muttock and Roddy Ray.

181. A former Tenant of Herm was Prince Blücher von Wahlstatt, who resided there from 1891 until 1914, when he was obliged to leave it because of his German nationality. During his tenancy he introduced wallabies to the island and one of them is seen in this photograph, taken before the First World War.

182. Herm wallabies seen in the deer park, an enclosure in the south of the island. It is believed that at one time there were as many as 25 wild animals there, as well as nine in the walled deer park. During the First World War a few soldiers were stationed in Herm and many were considerably startled on sentry duty when wallabies suddenly sprang out of the darkness onto the path! The animals appear to have died out soon afterwards.

83. These two graves, situated beside the road leading from Herm's harbour to the common, stand in a railed enclosure close to the shore. They are in memory of K. W. Conden, aged two years, and R. Mansfield, aged 33 years, who died in April 1832. In that year, a German ship was anchored off St Peter Port with the bodies of two cholera victims aboard. Since the town authorities refused them burial, the vessel sailed to Herm and her captain paid the quarrymen there to construct a little graveyard for their burial.

84. The States Board of Administration in Herm in 1949, not long after Guernsey had purchased the island from the Crown. From left to right are: Jurat Pierre le Putron, Jurats W. J. Sarre and Ernest le Garis, Louis Guillemette (assistant supervisor), H. E. Marquand (supervisor), Mr. L. R. Cohen (?), R. W. Hunkin (supervisor's secretary) and E. F. Lainé (the States engineer).

Jethou

185.   The children of Mr. and Mrs. Angus Faed, previously Crown Tenant of Jethou, in 1970. From left to right are Colin (12), Eric (10), Colette (8) and Amanda (7). They are seated on an old gun which faced out to sea towards Guernsey. Herm can be seen in the background. In 1971 the Faeds forsook the island because of the problem of educating their children. For a time they had resident tutors and also received tuition in Guernsey. The Herm school, unfortunately, was unsuitable because of the problem of ferrying them over La Percée passage daily. Sir Charles and Lady Hayward succeeded the Faed family in 1971 and remained in possession of the island for 12 years. In 1984, the lease was sold to Mr. Anthony George Duckworth.

6. The signboard of Jethou's one and only public house, *The Admiral Restald*, set up by Group-Captain W. H. Cliff during his tenancy. The board was painted by Charles ?ker, a Guernsey artist, and shows what Cliff described as ?hou's first tenant. Restald held the island from 1032 until ?70, after which the island passed into the hands of the ?bot of Mont St Michel. The pub ceased to function when ? tenancy changed hands in 1968.

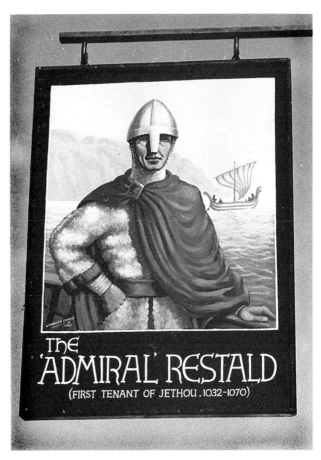

7. Crown Tenant of Jethou, Group Captain W. H. Cliff, ?n behind the bar of his public house, *The Admiral Restald*. ?stald is believed to have been shipmaster of William the ?nqueror and was granted the island as a reward for his ?aritime services. Group Capt. Cliff was in Jethou from 1962 ?til 1968. In the first year of his tenancy, he went to the ?umps reef, north of Herm, with geologist Dudley ?tenborough, to study rock formations. On their return to ?hou, their boat overturned and both fell overboard. For ?urs they clung to the upturned craft, then ?r. Attenborough let go of his hold and was drowned. His ?mpanion clung on, however, and eventually a passing ?unch rescued him.

188.   During the Faed regime in Jethou, a rather precarious-looking wooden jetty was used, although only when the tide was suitable. Fred Zabiela can be seen in the launch *Lady June*, using the jetty in 1964 at low tide. The Faeds had their own launch to convey passengers and cargo between the island and Guernsey. When Sir Charles Hayward became tenant a more substantial jetty was built.

189. Tail-piece.

A striking impression of Alderney's breakwater, painted by George Reynolds in 1852. A good deal of the mole had been completed, the work having begun in 1847. In the foreground, trains drawn by both a locomotive and horses are conveying stone to the breakwater and there are several ships in the New Harbour, as well as in the roadstead. At the time, 1,300 ft. of the mole had been built; its final length was approximately 3,500 ft.